$25-

GREAT BUDDHIST STORIES

BUDDHA
and his friends

S. DHAMMIKA
&
SUSAN HARMER

TIMES BOOKS INTERNATIONAL
Singapore • Kuala Lumpur

Ven. S. Dhammika was born in Australia in 1951. He was ordained as a Buddhist monk in India and later lived in Sri Lanka where he became well known for his efforts to promote Buddhism. In 1985, he moved to Singapore to become spiritual advisor to the Buddha Dhamma Mandala Society, a post he held until 1992 when he returned to Sri Lanka. Ven. Dhammika has written numerous books and made several television films on Buddhism.

Susan Harmer was born in Singapore in 1955. She taught music in England for many years before returning to Singapore in 1989 to embark on a career as an illustrator. Since then, she has worked extensively in both advertising and publishing. She now spends her time equally between teaching music and illustrating books. Her keen interest in Buddhism has led her to collaborate with Ven. Dhammika on *Great Buddhist Stories: Buddha and His Friends*.

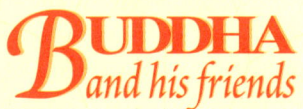

Text by Valerie Lauw

© 1997 Ven. S. Dhammika and Susan Harmer
Reprinted 1998

Published by Times Books International
an imprint of Times Editions Pte Ltd
Times Centre
1 New Industrial Road
Singapore 536196
Fax: (65) 2854871 Tel: (65) 2848844
E-mail: te@corp.tpl.com.sg
Online Book Store: http://www.timesone.com.sg/te

Times Subang
Lot 46, Subang Hi-Tech Industrial Park
Batu Tiga
40000 Shah Alam
Selangor Darul Ehsan
Malaysia
Fax & Tel: (603) 7363517
E-mail: cchong@tpg.com.my

All rights reserved. No part of this publication may be reproduced, stored in a retrieval system or transmitted, in any form or by any means, electronic, mechanical, photocopying, recording or otherwise, without the prior permission of the copyright owner.

Printed in Singapore

ISBN 981 204 634 8

Contents

1. A Prince is Born 4
2. Growing Up 10
3. Renouncing the World 15
4. Searching for the Truth 22
5. Prince Siddattha Becomes the Buddha 27
6. Sunita the Outcast 33
7. Tissa the Sick Monk 36
8. The Unlucky Cloak 39
9. Angulimala 42
10. The Angry Brahmin 51
11. The Mustard Seed 54
12. Trouble on the Rohini 57

A Prince Is Born

Long ago in ancient India, near the foothills of the Himalayas, was the land of the Sakyans and their beautiful city, Kapilavatthu. Their king was Suddhodana.

He had two wives - Maha Maya and Mahapajapati Gotami.

One night as Maha Maya lay sleeping...

Oh, what a strange dream! I must tell the king tomorrow morning!

A white elephant! How auspicious! This means something good is about to occur!

Some weeks later...

You were right about my dream. I'm going to have a baby!

That's wonderful!

Then one day...

Sire, I'd like to leave for my parents' home soon. As is our custom, I'd like to have the baby there and it's due any time now.

Then you shall leave tomorrow.

Growing Up

Renouncing The World

When Prince Siddattha came of age, he was married to a beautiful princess named Yasodhara.

"From now on, this palace will be your home. I will see to it that you will never want for anything!"

The young couple's life seemed perfect.

"They are so happy! Asita was wrong... Siddattha will be king one day!"

Having given up his princely possessions, Siddattha walked alone into the world.

The End

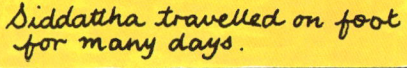

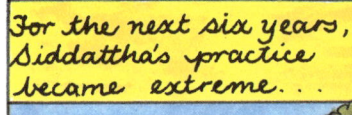

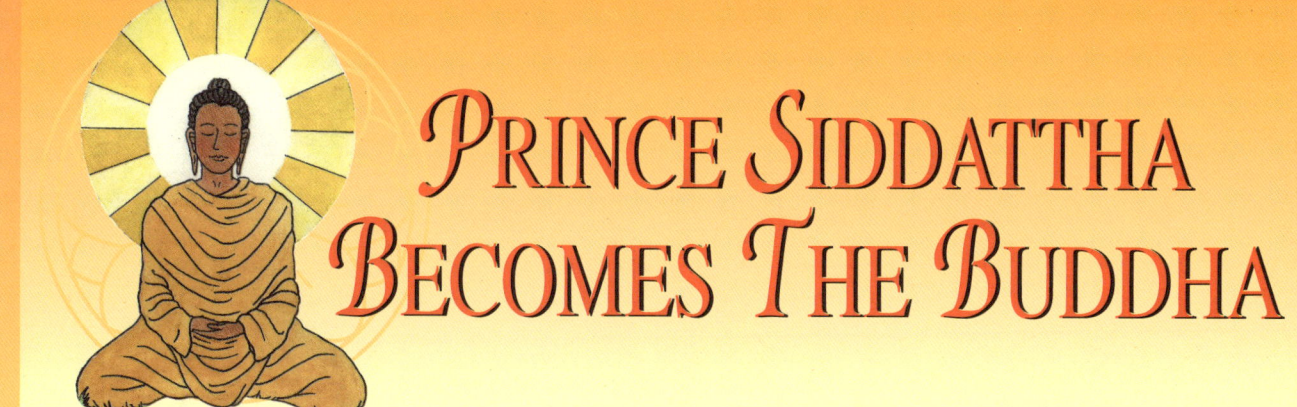

PRINCE SIDDATTHA BECOMES THE BUDDHA

Then.
"Mara* is coming!"
*Mara - the Evil One.

"Now let's have some fun!"

"Why waste your time with all this meditation? Take this jewel and fulfill all your wishes!"
"Be still, it is only Mara!"

"Not tempted? How about this woman? Take her and satisfy all your desires!"
"You cannot tempt me, Mara!"

"I'm impressed... his mind is strong! But I know what no one can resist!"

Sunita The Outcast

- Look, an outcast! Let's go the other way.

- Hey, outcast, get rid of this rubbish!

- Pooh! That rubbish heap stinks!

- What a start to the day! I'll just sit here and rest for a moment!

- Begone, outcast and don't come near my door again!

33

Filthy fellow!

What a life! I'm condemned to sweep the streets for the rest of my days...

...and because of that, people look down on me!

Come away from that man. He's an outcast!

Would you like more rice, dear?

How lovely it would be to live in a nice house, have a good job and be liked by others!

But I must stop daydreaming. It only makes me feel worse.

Ah! It's the Buddha!

But he won't want to see a wretched creature like me. I'll go somewhere else!

Funny! There he is again!

I'll go down this lane instead!

I don't believe it. How can this be?

It's strange. He seems to be everywhere!

I must try and keep out of his way.

I'll go in the opposite direction. Surely then I won't bump into him!

| | "Oh, Lord Buddha! I'm sorry! Please forgive me. I can't understand what's happening!" | "Sunita! I get the feeling you're trying to avoid me." |

"Oh, no Lord... I mean, yes, Lord! I'm an outcast. Look at how dirty I am. That's why I have to stay away from people."

"Come with me. I want to show you something!" / "Just a minute! How did he know my name?"

"Bathe in the river, Sunita!"

"This man has a good heart but because of his low caste, he thinks he is worthless."

"Look at yourself! You're as clean as anyone else!"

"It doesn't matter how dirty you are or even what job you do. What matters is the state of your mind. It only takes soap and water to clean the body..."

"...but to purify the mind you need to practise the Dhamma."

Later... "I have listened to your words, Lord, and I've decided to become a monk and join the Sangha."

"I'm happy to hear that!"

The End

TISSA THE SICK MONK

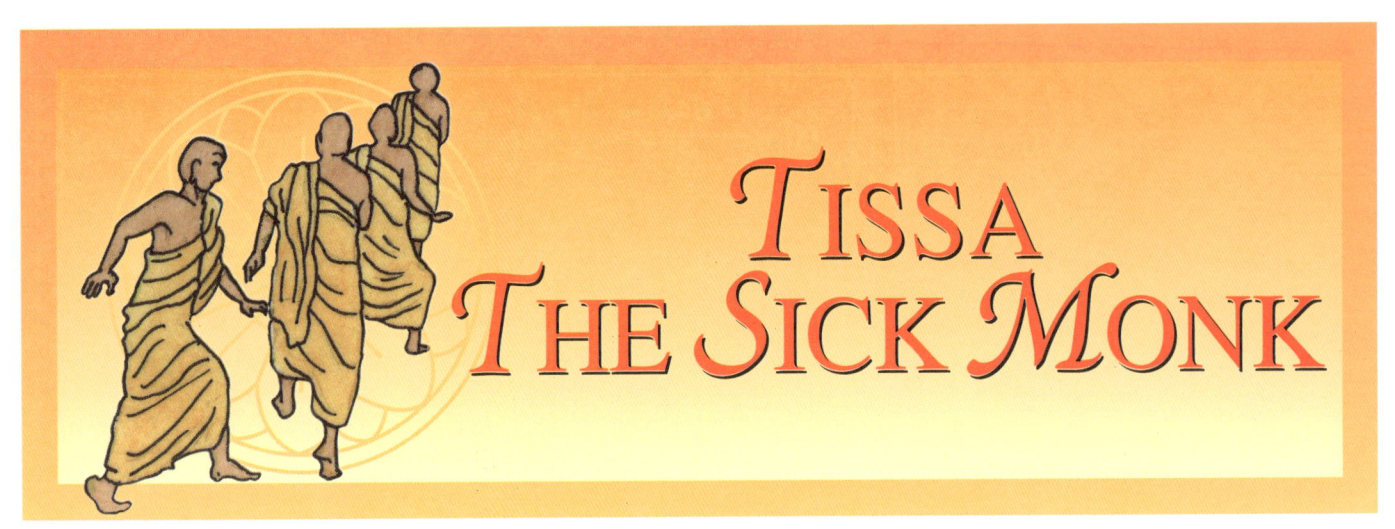

Panel 1: Tissa makes sure we have fresh water every day. What would we do without him?

Panel 2 – One day... Oh, bother! Not a drop left! Where's Tissa?

Panel 3 – The next day... I'm sorry about the lack of water yesterday but I wasn't feeling very well. Don't worry.

Panel 4: We've organised someone else to do the job whenever you're not around.

Panel 5 – A few weeks later... I haven't seen Tissa around for a while. Where is he?

Panel 6: I don't know. I think he's ill again. Perhaps you ought to go and see if he needs anything.

Panel 7: Not today. We've got far too much to do. Why don't you go?

Panel 8: Actually, I've also got a lot to do today. I'll go and see him tomorrow if I'm not too busy.

Tissa was seen less and less. But because there was always fresh water, no one missed him.

One day...

Come, Ananda. Let's pay the monks here a visit.

Aughh...

Look at the state he's in! How awful!

Help me carry him out into the fresh air!

Bring some water!

The Buddha! I didn't know he was here!

"I'd better tell the others!"	"You are clean now. How do you feel?"	"Much better, thank you, Lord!"

"Welcome, Lord. What a wonderful surprise it is to see you!"

"Why has this monk been left to lie in his own filth?"

"We didn't know he was so ill! We were going to visit him but something always came up!"

"And he never said he needed help!"

"Would things have been different if it had been me?"

"Oh, yes, Lord!"

"I mean... no, Lord... I mean ... oh dear..."

"Let's be truthful about this. Once Tissa was of no use to us, we never even thought about him."

"Monks, you no longer have a family. If you don't look after each other, who will? Those who would care for me should also care for the sick!"

The End

THE UNLUCKY CLOAK

According to my horoscope, it should be safe to leave the house today.

I think I'll go for a walk.

"Servant! Bring me my cloak!" "Yes, master."

"Oh no, mice!"

They've gnawed a hole in it! Oh dear, the Master will be angry when I tell him!

"A mouse did what? Let me see that!"

"According to the shape and location of such holes, you can predict whether the person who wears it will have bad or good luck!"

"Oh, how inauspicious! Whoever wears this cloak will meet with disaster!"

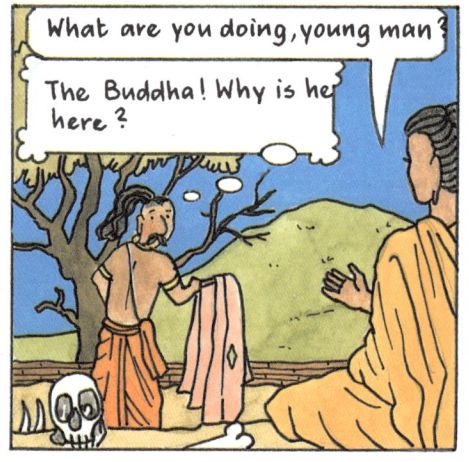

"Servant! Take that cursed thing to the cemetery and leave it there!" / "But that's your best cloak!"	"So it is! He'll never throw away such an expensive cloak. He'll probably hide it in his room and bring disaster to the whole household!"	"Son, you do it instead."
	"And make sure you have a bath after you've got rid of it!" / "Yes, father!"	*The Buddha saw all this with his supernormal powers.* "This Brahmin could understand the Dhamma if only he wasn't so superstitious. I will help him."
	"What are you doing, young man?" / "The Buddha! Why is he here?"	"I'm throwing away this cloak, Lord. A mouse chewed an unlucky hole in it."
"I'm in need of cloth for a new robe. I'll take it."	"Even to touch such a thing will mean disaster. I beg you not to use it, Lord."	"Good or bad luck cannot come from holes in cloth."

Panel	Text
1	This is terrible! I must tell father!
2	Oh my goodness! Quick! Get some good cloth and come with me!
3	The Buddha doesn't know what he's doing! Let's hope we're not too late!
4	Lord! Stop! Great harm will befall you if you wear that cloak!
5	Brahmin, a hole is just empty space. How can empty space harm anyone?
6	Well,... I'm not sure...
7	Wise people understand that evil comes from doing evil, and good comes from doing good.
8	Mmmh... that does make sense...
9	...he's right, I have been acting foolishly!
10	Lord, if you can use that cloak without fear, so can I. I'll take it back and give you the new cloth.
11	I can hardly believe my eyes!
12	Thank you, Lord. You have taught me much!
13	Put aside your superstitions. Hold fast to good deeds and you'll live free from fear.

The End

ANGULIMALA

King Pasenadi had a superstitious chaplain named Bhaggava Gagga.

Husband dear, we have a son.

What a lovely baby!

I'll check his horoscope.

Oh no! It says he will grow up to be very violent!

Isn't there anything we can do?

Perhaps there is. First we must give him the right name.

We'll call him Ahimsaka. It means 'harmless'. That should help.

As time passed... He's growing into a fine boy. But we must be careful. You know what his horoscope said.

Ahimsaka, you must do what I tell you without question!

Yes, father! Always!

Good! Remember that!

One day . . .
I've decided to send you to Taxila for further studies.
Don't forget what I've told you!
I know. I must be obedient and do whatever my teacher says.
Later in Taxila . . .
Are you the new student?
Yes, teacher. I am Ahimsaka.
Good. You can stay in my house and wait upon me. In return, I'll teach you all the arts and sciences. Now go join the others.
Thank you, sir.
During lessons . . .
Good answer, Ahimsaka!
After many months . . .
Correct again, Ahimsaka. That's all for today.
Who told you to stack those writing boards?
You did, sir!
So I did. Run along now!
Yes, sir!
Hmm . . . he's a good student and he does everything I tell him. That's unusual for a boy his age. I wonder what he's really up to . . .
Come into town with us, Ahimsaka. We know where they'll sell us alcohol. We're going to have a wild time!
I can't. I have work to do.
No, you don't, there's no homework tonight!
But I have to clean the teacher's room and run some errands for him.

- What a goody goody!
- ♪ Teacher's pet! Teacher's pet! ♪
- I told you it was a waste of time asking him!
- Let's teach him a lesson!
- I've got an idea! Listen...

That night...
- He said he was going to get rid of the teacher?
- Yes, his father knows the King so it shouldn't be difficult!
- Who's out there?

- Were they talking about me?

The next day...
- What's this? Looks like a letter from Ahimsaka to his father!
- He's reading it! Great!

- So! This young man intends to get me the sack, does he? We'll see about that!

Later...
- Ahimsaka! What are you doing going through my things?
- But one of the other students said...
- Never mind, I don't want to know. You've been here two years now. Your education is finished. I want my fee!
- Yes, sir!

Bring me the first finger from the hands of a thousand people!
WHAT? You can't mean that!
I am your teacher and you must do as I say! Now go!
I... I... but...
And don't you dare return without them!
Yes, sir.
Long before he gets all the fingers, someone will kill him and I'll never have to see him again!
I don't want to do this but what choice do I have?
First I must find somewhere to stay.
This forest cave looks like a good hideout.
That night...
Finger number one!
After some months...
This makes sixteen! It's not as bad as I thought.
For the first time in my life, I'm in charge!
One day...
What the...

Shoo! Shoo! Get out of my cave, you wretched things!

They've eaten the other fingers! I'll have to start from scratch. How can I prevent this happening again?

I know! I'll string them around my neck. Then I can keep count and I won't lose them either!

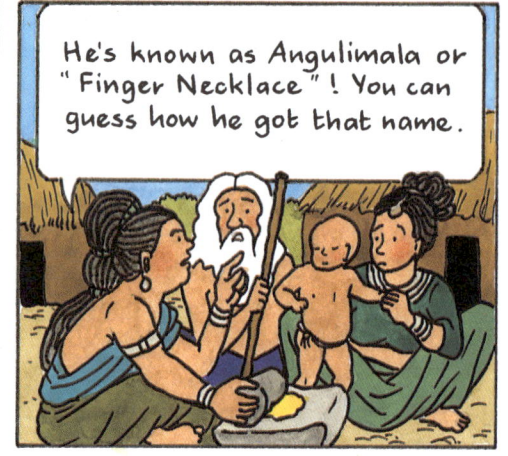

After some time...
This is much better!

Thereafter...
If you're travelling on the Savatthi road, be careful. There's a notorious killer at large!

He's known as Angulimala or "Finger Necklace"! You can guess how he got that name.

Meanwhile, in Savatthi...
King Pasenadi! Are you going into battle?

No, Lord. We're going to capture a murderer called Angulimala who's operating in these forests.

For your own safety, please don't go anywhere on your own.

I've heard of this man. Thank you for your concern.

Sometime later...

Who's there?

Oh, thank goodness it's only the Buddha!

Panel 1: "Please be careful, Lord. That murderer could be anywhere in this area!" / "I will."

Panel 2: "Angulimala is causing great suffering to others and to himself. Perhaps I can help him."

Panel 3: "Ah... I sense his presence."

Panel 4: "It's the Buddha and he's alone! I'll kill him and cut off one of his fingers!"

Panel 5: "I'll strike him down just before that next bend!"

Panel 6: "Whew! He walks too fast! I'll try again."

Panel 7: "I don't believe this is happening..."

Panel 8: "...I'm running as fast as I can and I still can't catch him!"

Panel 9: (no text)

Panel 10: "Gasp... it's no good... I can't keep this up!"

47

STOP!

But I have stopped, Angulimala. It is you who have not stopped!

Huh? What does he mean?

I have stopped harming living beings. It's time you stopped harming them too!

What have I done?

Oh, Lord, my life is so wretched and miserable I don't know what to do!

Please help me!

Come, let us leave this place.

Back in Savatthi, the Buddha taught Angulimala the Dhamma.

Later... Devadatta, please attend to this new monk.

It's Angulimala!

Does the Buddha think this is a refuge for criminals? Look at him... he can't have washed for months!

| Panel 1 | Panel 2 | Panel 3 |

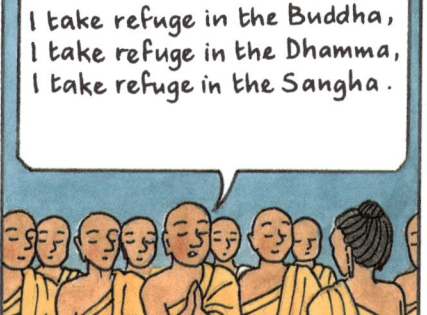

"Put that part over your shoulder. At least now you'll look like a monk."

"I take refuge in the Buddha, I take refuge in the Dhamma, I take refuge in the Sangha."

The next day... "Greetings, Lord, I've just returned."
"Did you find that murderer?"

"No, but I came within inches of catching him. Next time he won't get away."

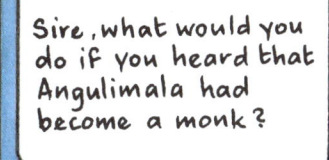

"Sire, what would you do if you heard that Angulimala had become a monk?"
"Impossible! These types never change!"

"But if he did, how would you receive him?"

"Well, I suppose if he had a change of heart and was truly sorry, I would bow to him as I would any other monk. Why?"

"Because this is Angulimala!"

"What?... you mean... he's...?"

"...well, Angulimala... I mean... Reverend Sir Angulimala, if you need anything,... anything at all,... just let me know..."

"The Buddha accomplished more with words than I could with spears and swords."

One day... "Isn't that Angulimala, the murderer?"
"It is him! I heard he became a monk!"

49

"Hey, you! Be off! You'll get nothing here!" "We don't want your type in this village!"

"You murderer! Go on... get out!"

"And never show your face here again!"

"It's the same wherever I go, Lord. People abuse and attack me!"

"This is the result of the evil you did in the past. Endure it with patience."

But in time, people came to accept Angulimala.

"It shows you people can change if they practise the Dhamma!"

The End

THE ANGRY BRAHMIN

It's good to be home again. Hmm... the village seems unusually quiet!

Hello, brother-in-law, what's the latest news?

Hi there, Asurinda! Welcome home!

I'll see you later.

What's the hurry? Can't we have a chat? I've only just got back.

Sorry, can't stop. Just off to see the Buddha. He's giving a sermon... almost everyone's going and I want a good seat!

Huh! Some welcome that was!

Further on...

Hi, neighbour! What's new?

Haven't you heard?

My daughter joined the Buddha's Sangha. The family's thrilled!

The Buddha again! You people are so boring!

Well, it's better than being grumpy like you!

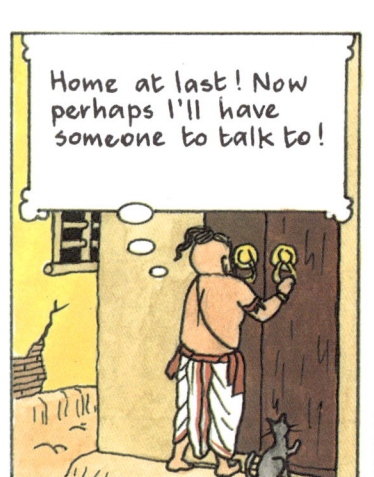

Panel 1: Home at last! Now perhaps I'll have someone to talk to!

Panel 2: Oh, hello, husband. We're on our way to the park, but we'll be back soon. We're going to hear the Buddha teach. The servant will get your lunch. Bye!

Panel 3: Come on, children! We don't want to be late!
Bye, father! But...

Panel 4: Welcome back, Master. I'll pour some water for you and then I'll be off.

Panel 5: And I suppose you're going to see the Buddha too!
Yes, that's right. He's going to talk about patience and kindness.

Panel 6: The Buddha this, the Buddha that! I'm sick of hearing about this fellow!

Panel 7: We'll see how patient and kind he is when I'm finished with him!

Panel 8: I'll give him a piece of my mind

Panel 9: I don't know why I work for him — look at this mess!

Panel 10: Get out of my way!
Shh!
Hey!

Panel 11: I want a word with you!
You can't talk to the Buddha like that!

52

Panel 1: I'll talk any way I want! SO MIND YOUR OWN BUSINESS!

Panel 2: AS FOR YOU...

Panel 3: There! What do you say to that?

Panel 4: Brahmin, do guests come to your home?
Of course! What's that got to do with this?

Panel 5: And do you serve them food and drink?
Yes, so what?

Panel 6: And if they refuse them, to whom do these things belong?
And if they don't accept my food and drink... er...

Panel 7: They belong to me, naturally!

Panel 8: Then, Brahmin, I refuse what you have given me. Your angry words belong to you. You can have them back!

Panel 9: ...
Now, as I was saying...

The End

The Mustard Seed

Kisa Gotami had a son.
"You're the most beautiful baby in the land!"

One day...
"Something is wrong. He's too quiet."

"He's not breathing!... oh, my son,... my only beloved son...!"

"You cannot die... I won't allow it!"

"I'm going to find some medicine to make you better!"

"Please help me... Where can I find medicine for my baby?"
!?

"Woman, your child is dead. There is no medicine for that!"
"What? NO!"

"Give him back to me!... I will find a cure for him!"

"Please can you help my baby?"

"Please help me..."
"Can't she see the poor child's dead?"

54

Cremate him and be done with it!
Come away, dear... she's obviously mad!
Poor woman, I feel so sorry for her!
Friend, the Buddha is staying outside the town. He is a great sage. If anyone can help you, he can!
Maybe he can bring my son back to life!
Get out of my way... I have to see the Buddha!
Lord Buddha, you have to help me...
After hearing her story...
Yes, Kisa Gotami, there is something you can do.
Whatever it is, I'll do it!
Bring me a mustard seed!
I will, I will... thank you, Lord!
But wait! It must come from a house where no one has ever died.
I don't get it! Why didn't he just tell her to accept that the baby is dead?
This shouldn't be too hard... soon my baby will be well again!
Grandmother, can you spare me a mustard seed?
Only one? Of course I can.

56

Panel 1: Oh, I nearly forgot. Has anyone ever died in this house?

Panel 2: Why, yes... my good husband died only last year.

Panel 3: Then this seed's no good!

Panel 4: *Further on...* Thank you for the mustard seed. Has anyone ever died in this house? — Our son... two summers ago.

Panel 5: This seed's no good either!

Panel 6: *After visiting many homes...* Several members of our family have died.

Panel 7: The living are few but the dead are many. There is not a single house where no one has died.

Panel 8: Death comes to everyone sooner or later. I was foolish to think that it should be different for my son.

Panel 9: *The next day...* Goodbye, my beloved one!

Panel 10: *Later...* Here's that woman again... but now she looks calm.

Panel 11: I've accepted my son's death now... and my grief is less. Your medicine has healed me. Thank you, Lord.

Panel 12: I get it... rather than make her face the truth, he gave her a task which allowed her to see it for herself.

Panel 13: What a wonderful teacher the Buddha is!

The End

Trouble on the Rohini

The Sakyans and the Koliyans were related. Their territory was divided by the Rohini River.

Both tribes had built a dam so they could irrigate their crops.

One day on the Sakyan side of the river...

"Whew! This must be one of the hottest summers we've ever had!"

"Let's go down to the river to get some water for the crops."

"Oh no! See how low the river is!"

"Never mind. The crops only need one more watering before they ripen and there's just enough for that. Let's get to work!"

Meanwhile, on the Koliyan side of the river...

"Our crops only need one more watering before they ripen."

"The river must be low after this long hot spell so let's go and get the water before the dam is empty."

"Look over there! It's the Koliyans. They're taking the water too."

"What if there's not enough water for all of us?"

"Come on, we'll have to stop them!"

Hey you Koliyans! Stop taking our water!
But we need it to water our crops.
So do we, and what's more . . .
. . . we were here first!
You weren't – we were!
First you take our water and now you call us liars!
Who do you think you're shoving?
What's going on?
I don't know but let's go back up our men!
You Koliyans live up trees like monkeys!
Ha! Ha! Ha!
Who are you calling 'monkeys'? You Sakyans are the monkeys, not us!
Then we'll show you how monkeys fight!
You'll be sorry you started this, Sakyans! We'll make you pay!
In the Koliyan capital of Devadaha . . .
We've just heard of a dispute on the Rohini involving the Sakyans. They insulted our people. Such behaviour cannot go unpunished!
I agree! We need to teach them a lesson. These Sakyans were always an arrogant lot! I say we call in the army!

And in the Sakyan capital of Kapilavatthu...

"Those Koliyans called our people 'monkeys'!"

"This means war!"

"Shouldn't we talk to them first?"

"This is not the time for talk... this is the time for action!"

"I agree! Let's teach them a lesson! Assemble the troops!"

Soon afterwards, the two armies faced each other, ready for battle.

Miles away...

"I sense trouble brewing. I must stop them before someone gets hurt."

"Get ready to attack! Death before dishonour!"

"Let's show these Sakyans how real warriors fight!"

"String your bows!"

"Draw your swords!"

Suddenly...

"Look, it's the Buddha! What's he doing here?"

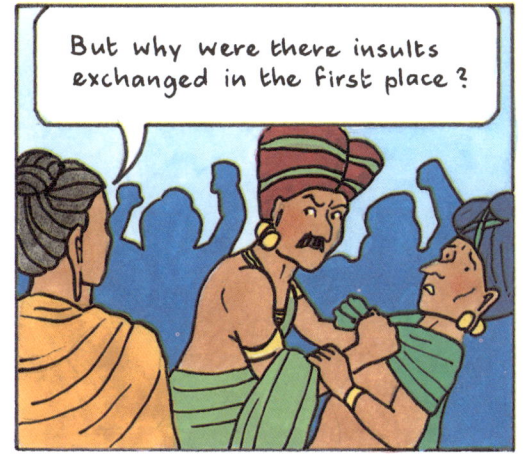

Hold your fire!

How did he appear just like that?

What's all this about?

They insulted us! — **No! They insulted us!**

If we insulted you, it's because you called us names first! — **No, you did!**

But why were there insults exchanged in the first place?

Well... er... — **...they... I... er...**

Don't look at me... I'm just a soldier... They told me to fight...

Panel 1: Then who would know? / Atula... he's Commander-in-Chief!

Panel 2: Summon Atula!

Panel 3: What is it? I'm busy discussing battle tactics with the Viceroy.

Panel 4: The Buddha wants a word with you, sir! / Oh, very well!

Panel 5: I hope he'll be brief. Our men are ready for battle! / Right!

Panel 6: You want to know why we are fighting? Well, I'll tell you... You see,... er... um...

Panel 7: ...Viceroy!... Why don't you answer? / Me?...well, I...

Panel 8: I suggest we ask the villagers.

Panel 9: Excellent idea, Lord! Why didn't I think of that? Bring them forward!

Panel 10: Lord, it's the water in the dam.

Panel 11: There's not enough for both our crops.

Panel 12: Tell me, what is more precious - water or human life?

Panel 13: Of course human life is more precious than water, Lord.

62

Then is it not foolish to kill people because of water?
And worse, you were ready to kill without even being sure of the reason!
Let me tell you a story . . .
. . . Once, there was a great storm . . .
. . The trees that grew close to each other and whose branches intertwined remained standing.
But a tree that grew alone and separate from the others . . .
. . . was blown down and destroyed!
Sakyans, Koliyans, settle your differences by talking, not fighting!
If you live in peace and unity, you will both prosper. Now, put away your weapons.
I live in peace and so can you.

"I suppose we could always share the water."

And so the Sakyans and the Koliyans learned to live in harmony. The harvest was bountiful and everyone was happy.

The End